the dreaming

by
Queenie Chan

HAMBURG // LONDON // LOS ANGELES // TOKYO

The Dreaming Vol. 1
Written and Illustrated by Queenie Chan

Production Artists - Lucas Rivera and Jason Milligan
Cover Design - Anne Marie Horne
Copy Editors - Peter Ahlstrom, Eric Althoff,
and Hope Donovan

Editor - Carol Fox
Digital Imaging Manager - Chris Buford
Production Managers - Jennifer Miller and Mutsumi Miyazaki
Managing Editor - Lindsey Johnston
VP of Production - Ron Klamert
Publisher and E.I.C. - Mike Kiley
President and C.O.O. - John Parker
C.E.O. - Stuart Levy

A **TOKYOPOP** Manga

TOKYOPOP Inc.
5900 Wilshire Blvd. Suite 2000
Los Angeles, CA 90036

E-mail: info@TOKYOPOP.com
Come visit us online at www.TOKYOPOP.com

ISBN: 1-4278-0005-7
First TOKYOPOP printing: August 2006
10 9 8 7 6 5 4 3 2 1
Printed in the USA

Table of Contents

For my
Mum
Susan,
and
my
Dad
Marco.

5

9

Chapter 1
A New School

19

EVERYONE, I'D LIKE YOU TO MEET--

-- YOUR TWO NIECES...

...THE *FAMOUS* AMBER AND JEANIE.

MRS. MALKIN TALKS ABOUT YOU TWO A *LOT*.

I'M SCHALA, NICE TO MEET YOU.

UH, *HI*...!

Chapter 2
The Door

WHAT'S TAKING THAT MILLIE GIRL SO LONG?

IT'S ALMOST NINE O'CLOCK!

WELL, I'M TAKING A WALK.

I'M NOT HUNGRY ANYWAY.

AH!

WAIT!

I'M COMING, TOO!

I DON'T WANT TO STAY HERE ALONE...

...? ...WHAT'S UP WITH YOU?

30

...A SEALED ROOM?

IT *LOOKS* LIKE IT'S BEEN SEALED FOR A WHILE...

I WONDER WHAT'S BEHIND THAT DOOR...

MILLIE!

AH!

FINALLY!

I WAS LOOKING ALL OVER FOR YOU TWO!

YOU...

...SHOUTED AT THE VICE-PRINCIPAL?!

...ARE YOU *CRAZY?*

UM... I, ER...

EVEN *I* WOULDN'T HAVE DARED TO DO THAT!

WELL, IT'S KINDA COOL, ACTUALLY.

42

FWAAA...

Chapter 3
The Dreaming

YOU GIRLS READY TO GO?

AH!

HEY, I'M TREVOR. A FRIEND OF MILLIE'S.

I'LL BE TAKING YOU TWO TO CLASS.

HA...

JEANIE...

IF YOU'RE NOT GOING TO READ THAT BOOK, JUST *RETURN* IT.

I AM GOING TO READ IT...

IT'S JUST THAT...

I DUNNO. I DON'T KNOW WHAT I'M GOING TO FIND IN THERE, THAT'S ALL.

WELL, JUST *RETURN* IT, THEN!

I DON'T KNOW ABOUT *YOU*, BUT THE DREAMS WE'VE BEEN HAVING...

...THEY *SCARE* ME.

WELL, NOTHING REALLY... *HAPPENS* IN THEM.

NO!

71

Chapter 4
The Mirror

79

87

NO...

NOTHING BUT A STREAM OF GARBLED LETTERS.

IT DIDN'T WORK.

ARE YOU *SURE* WE'RE DOING THIS RIGHT?

PRETTY SURE.

WELL ...

MAYBE THOSE GIRLS WHO VANISHED IN THE BUSH JUST DON'T WANT TO TALK TO US THIS TIME.

EH? YOU MEAN...

...YOU WERE TRYING TO COMMUNICATE WITH THOSE GIRLS THROUGH THE SEANCE?

YUP!

WE WANT TO KNOW WHAT *REALLY* HAPPENED TO THEM.

99

Chapter 5
The Vice-Principal

OH, I SEE ...

WELL, GOOD LUCK. TELL ME ABOUT IT LATER.

W-WHAT ....?

AREN'T YOU COMING WITH US ....?

LOOK, IF MISS ANU DIDN'T MENTION ME, THEN THIS ISN'T REALLY MY PROBLEM!

HOW CAN YOU SAY THAT?!

WHAT?! ME? WHAT FOR?!

I'M NOT THE ONE WHO'S IN TROUBLE!

I'M JUST ASKING IF YOU CAN COME ALONG!

AFTER ALL, IT WAS BECAUSE OF YOURS AND MILLIE'S PARTY THAT--

WAIT...

OH. SO THAT'S IT!

HMM...

HEY, PEOPLE!

THIS DOOR'S NOT SHUT PROPERLY EITHER.

YOU THINK SHE MIGHT BE IN THERE?

I GUESS WE CAN GIVE IT A SHOT...

WELL, IT BEATS STANDING AROUND WAITING.

TRY IT?

YUP!

NOW WAIT A SECOND!

WE SHOULDN'T BE HERE IN THE FIRST PLACE-- OPEN DOOR OR NOT!

123

Chapter 6
Circle

I WOKE UP IN THE MIDDLE OF THE NIGHT TO FIND HER BED EMPTY.

I WOKE UP AGAIN A FEW HOURS LATER, AND SHE STILL HADN'T RETURNED...

I WAITED AT LEAST HALF AN HOUR FOR HER, BUT...

WELL, I HAVEN'T SEEN HER. I WAS *ASLEEP*, SHEESH!

I CAME HERE TO SEE WHETHER *YOU* WERE STILL IN BED...

...BUT YOU APPEARED TO BE HAVING A *NIGHTMARE* OF SOME SORT...

145

149

Chapter 7
Reflection

SO THAT'S WHAT WE DID, WORRY GNAWING AT THE CORNERS OF OUR MINDS.

AND SO WE WAITED...

...AND WAITED...

...UNTIL THE SUN ROSE.

AND SO THE SUN SET...

...ON YET ANOTHER DAY.

161

The Dreaming: Volume II...

With Millie's death, the school grinds completely to a halt.
As many students return home, fearful rumours are
whispered in the halls, and a dark, ominous cloud seems to
descend upon the school. Unable to leave and still plagued by
her dreams, Jeanie attempts to discover more about the other
missing girls. As she begins to delve into the history of the
school, she realizes just how dark and disturbing its past
really is...

The Inspiration for "The Dreaming"

Australia has many stories involving schoolgirls vanishing into the bush. Perhaps the most famous one is a 1967 novel by Joan Lindsay called *Picnic at Hanging Rock*, later made into a movie. The book caused quite a stir when first released, as readers believed the events described in the book were true. This was unlikely, but the story captured the public imagination—largely because such stories often have some basis in fact.

However, my inspiration for *The Dreaming* doesn't really come from this book. It comes more directly from a former classmate of mine, class of '97, who vanished in the Tasmanian wilderness while trekking from one point to another. She was alone, and wasn't following any trails, but had made the trip before, so her disappearance wasn't due to inexperience—or suicide. They found her camping gear, all set up for the night, but despite searching everywhere for miles around, they found no trace of her. Months later, she was pronounced "missing, presumed dead."

I wonder what happened to her sometimes. Did she run into someone else out there, in the middle of nowhere? Did she fall into some hidden crevice, and the earth just swallowed her up? Perhaps, when I wrote this story, I was trying to explain something that really has no explanation.

Thousands of people go missing every year, in many countries, for no discernable reason most of the time. Most of these people are never seen again, and what happens to them remains an unsolved mystery. What are the chances it could be someone you know...or you?

Amber and Jeanie hail from an earlier pitch of mine to TOKYOPOP—*TwinSide*, which can be found at *www.queeniechan.com*. It was a romantic comedy, but hey...things change.

Truth is, they have an even earlier incarnation, in a short story I drew for a competition, called *Twins* (also on my site). I often build long stories from my short stories, and vice versa. It's a good way of establishing the characters and their world before a longer story. *Twins* is nothing like *The Dreaming*, but you may find the girls still retain some remnants of their old personalities.

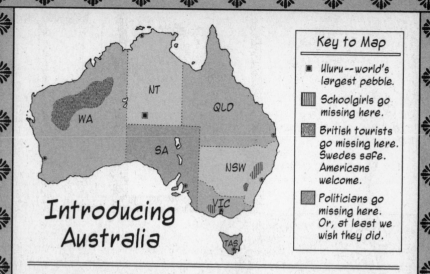

Introducing Australia

Key to Map

- ▪ Uluru--world's largest pebble.
- ▥ Schoolgirls go missing here.
- ▦ British tourists go missing here. Swedes safe. Americans welcome.
- ▨ Politicians go missing here. Or, at least we wish they did.

Australia is a rather young country, with a history of about 200 years. It was first "discovered" in 1770 by an English fella called Captain James Cook, who recognised its excellent potential as a convict dumping ground. There were already native Aborigines living here, but they were regarded merely as part of the local wildlife and thus ignored (the lucky ones, that is).

Over time, the country became independent and formed a federation of states. They are New South Wales, Victoria, Queensland, South Australia, Northern Territory, Western Australia, Tasmania and the Australian Capital Territory. Naturally, the country has long stopped importing criminals, though many criminals still work in the government.

AUSTRALIA

This is the esteemed Australian coat-of-arms, flanked by the Kangaroo and the Emu. Come to think of it, we shoot and eat both these animals.

BET YOU DIDN'T KNOW...

For a multi-cultural country, Australia has one of the world's leading diasporas--5% of the total population. 1 million Aussies live and work overseas.

Multiple Choice Question: The Australian outback is crawling with:

a) sheep and other cattle
b) serial killers
c) foreign tourists convinced they're experiencing the "real" Australia
d) all of the above

Answer: (d)

Locker No. 246

By Sarah Ferrick

AN ECCENTRIC GIRL AND HER FRUSTRATED BEST FRIEND
FORM THE HEART OF THIS DARKLY HUMOROUS STORY,
WRITTEN AND ILLUSTRATED BY ONE OF TOKYOPOP'S
FORMER RISING STARS OF MANGA WINNERS. SARAH
FERRICK'S SHORT MANGA IS THE FIRST IN AN ONGOING
SERIES OF ORIGINAL BACKUP FEATURES THAT WILL BE
EXCLUSIVE TO TOKYOPOP'S ORIGINAL MANGA. ENJOY!

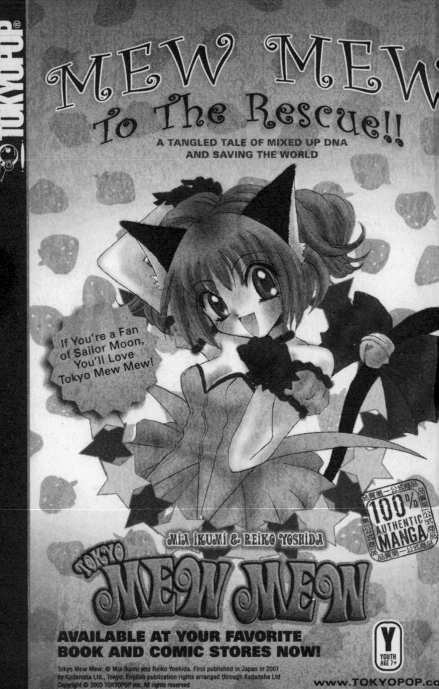